THE
EVER-WINNING
FAITH

DAVID B. OSHO

THE EVER-WINNING FAITH

Copyright © Year 2021 by David B. Osho

ISBN: 978-1-952098-89-5

Published by:

Cornerstone Publishing
A Division of Cornerstone Creativity Group LLC
Info@thecornerstonepublishers.com
www.thecornerstonepublishers.com

Author's Contact

For booking to speak at your next event or to order bulk copies of this book, please send email to:

oshodb@yahoo.com

DEDICATION

To the One Who is, Who was and Who is to come,
The Almighty God. Truly, He is the One Who raises
the poor from the dust and lifts the needy from the ash
heap to make them sit with princes

To my second-half, Pastor Esther Osho, Who I fondly
called "Honey Me". You have been there with me
through thick and thin. I celebrate your unrelenting
support and love. I cherish your companionship.

Finally, I dedicate this book to those who love Jesus, the
Author and the Finisher Of our Faith.

CONTENTS

INTRODUCTION

FAITH TO WIN IN THE BATTLES OF LIFE

There is something in you capable of subduing any challenges you face. There is a power at work inside of you capable of overcoming any trouble, obstacle, or enemy; it is the force of your faith.

Regardless of the magnitude of your challenges, or battles, if faith is in place, you can come out a winner. I mean, every single time! Amazingly, faith does not just give you the victory, faith is the victory.

The scriptures say, "...For whatsoever is born of God overcometh the world: and this is the victory that overcometh the world, even our faith." (1 John 5:4)

You need faith to confront and conquer all the challenges of life. Faith in God is one of the most powerful forces on earth. Your faith is your life jacket; without it, you will drown. Your faith is your weapon, without it, you will be defeated. Faith is what ushers in the supernatural power of God in your life and delivers victory to you. Every time victory is obtained, faith was exercised. Likewise, every time there is defeat, faith was absent. Without faith, you will become a victim of life's many challenging circumstances. But with The Ever-Winning Faith, all the possibilities of divinity become your present reality.

The battles of life are inevitable. No matter how hard you try to avoid them, they will still come to you. As long as you are alive, you will encounter troubles and challenges. But whenever you face challenges, rather than give up or run, see it as your greatest opportunity to see God manifest, not just in your life but in your circumstances. The truth is, faith is at its best in the face of challenges.

If you go to Hebrews chapter 11, you will read about the mighty men and women of faith who conquered their obstacles by virtue of the force of faith. Their stories are not without fearful experiences, but their faith brought them supernatural victory nonetheless.

"And what more shall I say? For the time would fail me to tell of Gideon and Barak and Samson and Jephthah, also of David and Samuel and the prophets: who through faith subdued kingdoms, worked righteousness, obtained promises, stopped the mouths of lions, quenched the violence of fire, escaped the edge of the sword, out of weakness were made strong, became valiant in battle, turned to flight the armies of the aliens. Women received their dead raised to life again. Others were tortured, not accepting deliverance, that they might obtain a better resurrection." (Hebrews 11:32-35)

The Ever-Winning Faith is, therefore, designed to equip and empower you to confront and overcome all the obstacles that life brings. Whenever you encounter any challenge, deploy your faith and come out a winner. The amazing thing is that each time you win in the battles of life, God receives the glory. Our constant victory is what puts the glory of God on public display. Hallelujah!

"Now thanks be unto God, which always causeth us to triumph in Christ, and maketh manifest the savor of his knowledge by us in every place." (2 Corinthians 2:14)

I tell you, if you believe the word of God if you will learn to stand strong on His promises, not only that you will enjoy victory over every battle; nothing shall be impossible to you!

—Pastor David B. Osho.

1

YOU ARE BORN A WINNER

In life, you will be confronted with a series of difficult challenges, battles, and obstacles; however, if you are born again, you have an advantage. In other words, you are bound to overcome. To be born again is to be born of God. That implies that the seed of God is inside you. The scripture tells us that a born-again child of God is not born by man's corruptible seed, but by the incorruptible seed of God Almighty.

"Being born again, not of corruptible seed, but of incorruptible, by the word of God, which liveth and abideth forever." 1 Peter 1:23

What that means is that you are born a winner. As a child of God, The DNA OF A WINNER IS INSIDE OF YOU. You have what it takes to dominate your circumstances, triumph over every trial, surmount every obstacle that may come your way. The new birth is what positions you as a winner.

"Whosoever believeth that Jesus is the Christ is born of

God: and every one that loveth him that begat loveth him also that is begotten of Him. By this, we know that we love the children of God when we love God and keep His commandments. For this is the love of God, that we keep his commandments: and His commandments are not grievous. For whatsoever is born of God overcometh the world: and this is the victory that overcometh the world, even our faith. Who is he that overcometh the world, but he that believeth that Jesus is the Son of God?" 1 John 5:1-5

KNOW WHO YOU ARE

The capacity to win is inside you. But unless you have a deep-seated revelation of who you are, you will be defeated. Your revelation is what decides your status..It is your discoveries in God that put you over the enemy and over every challenge that you are confronted with in life. If you are ignorant, the enemy will keep molesting you. In fact, your ignorance gives the devil an advantage over you.

"Lest Satan should get an advantage of us: for we are not ignorant of his devices." 2 Corinthians 2:11

YOU ARE A GOD

You have to understand that as a child of God, you share in the same status with God. In other words, you are a god. First, your new birth experience empowers you with the right to be a son of God (John 1:12); and by virtue of being a son, you are a god. The implication of that is that you carry God's capacity in you. That is why God did not only declare us His offsprings but also gave us the responsibility to exercise dominion over the forces of oppression, and put them where they belong.

"God standeth in the congregation of the mighty; he judgeth among the gods. How long will ye judge unjustly, and accept the persons of the wicked? Selah.

Defend the poor and fatherless: do justice to the afflicted and needy. Deliver the poor and needy: rid them out of the hand of the wicked." Psalm 82:1-4

Even Jesus affirmed this truth when He boldly declared: "...Is it not written in your law, I said, Ye are gods? If He called them gods, unto whom the word of God came, and the scripture cannot be broken." John 10:34

However, if you are ignorant of who you are and what belongs to you, you will be defeated like an ordinary man who does not have access to the God-life. This is a tragedy!

"They know not, neither will they understand; they walk on in darkness: all the foundations of the earth are out of course. I have said, Ye are gods, and all of you are children of the highest. But ye shall die like men, and fall like one of the princes." Psalm 82:5-7

It is through the knowledge of the word that we became PARTAKERS of the divine nature. Although you are already a son of God by virtue of the new birth but by revelations, you partake in its reality.

"Grace and peace be multiplied unto you through the knowledge of God, and of Jesus our Lord, According as his divine power hath given unto us all things that pertain unto life and godliness, through the knowledge of Him that hath called us to glory and virtue: Whereby are given unto us exceeding great and precious promises: that by these ye might be partakers of the divine nature, having escaped the corruption that is in the world through lust." 2 Peter 1:2-4

If you lack this fundamental understanding, you will be a theoretical victor, having only head knowledge, but lacking the experience in your life. But once you catch that revelation, you automatically escape the corruption and the limitations that are common to all the unbelievers in this world. In other words, you begin to live way above all the battles and challenges of life.

YOU ARE FROM ABOVE

If you are born again, you are from above; you do not only exist on earth but in a realm higher than the earth—the spirit realm. You are not just a body, you are a spirit and the life in the spirit is above all the limitations in the earthly realm. This was exactly what Jesus taught in the third chapter of John's gospel.

"Jesus answered, Verily, verily, I say unto thee, Except a man be born of water and of the Spirit, he cannot enter into the kingdom of God. That which is born of the flesh is flesh, and that which is born of the Spirit is spirit. Marvel not that I said unto thee, Ye must be born again. The wind bloweth where it listeth, and thou hearest the sound thereof, but canst not tell whence it cometh, and whither it goeth: so is every one that is born of the Spirit." John 3:5-8

Any believer who understands this fact cannot be defeated or limited by anything, no matter what it is. No obstacle, problem, or challenge can drown you because you are a spirit from above. You are practically invisible!

"He that cometh from above is above all: he that is of the earth is earthly, and speaketh of the earth: he that cometh from heaven is above all." John 3:31

ALL THINGS UNDER YOUR FEET

You must have to identify with His finished works to operate at the same level of invincibility as Jesus. Whatever Jesus did, He did not just for you but as you. He died our death so that we can live His life. When He died, I died with Him, when He was buried, I was buried with Him; when He rose, I rose with Him, when He ascended, I ascended with Him. When He was seated, I was seated with Him...at the right hand of God Almighty, "...Far above all principality, and power, and might, and dominion, and every name that is named, not only in this world but also in that which is to come. And hath put all things under His feet, and gave Him to be the head over all things to the church, Which is His body, the fullness of Him that filleth all in all." Ephesians 1:18-23 (Emphasis mine).

In a nutshell, Jesus became all that we were, so that we can become all that He is. And the scripture rightly tells us that as He is in heaven (above all obstacles), so are we in this world (1 John 4:17). You cannot be defeated because, not only that you are from above, but more so because all things have been put under your feet. You have already defeated and overcome every battle and forces of darkness that could have defeated you. You are way ahead of all your enemies. And as you take your place in the body of Christ and run the race you were born to run, your winning is inevitable. How could you be defeated by something that is under your feet?

YOU ARE IN GOD'S TEAM

One of the easiest ways to win in life is to join the winning team. If you are in the losing team, no matter what you do, you are still a loser. But if you are on the winning team, no matter what, you'll win! Amazingly, we are born again into an ever-winning team—a team that never losses any battles. This team is made up of God the Father, the Son, the Holy Spirit, and His family; with God the Father as our leader. And like the Bible tells us, all powers and forces submit to Him.

16

That means, there is no circumstances or situation that can defile His power and authority. God's side is always the winning side. If God is for you, it doesn't matter who is against you, you will have victory over them (Romans 8:31). You can never lose with God on your side!

As part of God's team, we are not fighting for victory, but from the position of victory. We were winners before ever we got in the battle. As a matter of fact, you cannot win unless you fight from the position of victory. In other words, victory is not our endpoint like many suppose, instead it is our very starting point.

NO MATTER WHAT, WE WIN!

You have to come to the point where you realize that a life of total victory is your birthright. You are born with a nature that cannot be overpowered or conquered by anything visible or invisible.

As a child of God, you are not a failure. God does not expect you to fail because He did not create you that way. And even when you experience failure, rather than see yourself as a failure, see failure as an event. Failure is not who you are, so when you fail, don't stay down, instead quickly get up, dust up yourself, and get going. Never give up simply because of temporary defeats in the form of failure. Always bear in mind that you are an offspring of the Almighty God and that every single thing you need to be a winner or to enjoy perpetual victory is not just at your disposal but inside of you.

Nevertheless, it is possible that you are already feeling discouraged. The challenges of life may have impacted you so much that you no longer look forward to winning but to hopelessness, despair, and defeat. In fact, the obvious realities of life may have pushed you to the point where you want to throw in the towel.

Well, I have good news for you. Despite all that you are going through and the challenging circumstances before you, you are still more than a conqueror. And if you are willing to take back the stirring of your life by faith, I guarantee, you will still emerge a winner.

As it is written, For thy sake we are killed all the day long; we are accounted as sheep for the slaughter. Nay, in all these things we are more than conquerors through him that loved us. Romans 8:36-37

Yes! IN ALL THESE THINGS WE ARE MORE THAN CONQUERORS!

So, while you are in the midst of battles and the challenges of life, realize you are more than a conqueror, through Jesus Christ.

FAITH IS YOUR TRUE VICTORY

Now, that's how faith works. Faith declares victory in the

midst of the battle because we are victorious in Christ. We are eternally established Victors and Winners, the battles notwithstanding.

2 Corinthians 2:14 says," Now thanks be unto God, which always causeth us to triumph in Christ…" In Christ we are triumphant. We don't quit, we win.

Regardless of the situation or challenge, you are facing right now, there is a supernatural force that is equal to the task. Without any doubt, this life force can solve any problem, no matter how difficult it may seem. Everything responds to this one supernatural force without exception. What could this vital supernatural force be? You may ask.

It is the force of faith. Faith in God is a very powerful force to alter the course of events on earth. It has the capacity to provoke significant progress in every area of your life. Faith can eliminate any obstacle before you, thereby paving way for you to get ahead in your endeavors. If you truly understand faith and how it works; I tell you, you will live in perpetual victory all the days of your life. When faith is in place, God is not only committed, he is compelled to perform his word.

"And blessed is she that believed: for there shall be a performance of those things which were told her from the Lord." Luke 1:45

The amazing thing about the force of faith is that it does

not only give us the victory, faith IS the victory. Faith is what it takes to make it happen!

THE MEASURE OF FAITH

As a child of God, you are born again into an ever-winning faith—faith capable of giving you victory over any prevailing circumstances of life. When you got born again, faith was born in your heart. The Bible tells us that we were given a measure of faith—a measure that is common to every new believer in Christ.

"For I say, through the grace given unto me, to every man that is among you, not to think of himself more highly than he ought to think; but to think soberly, according to as God hath dealt with every man the measure of faith." Romans 12:3

This faith is like your startup capital to live a life of total victory over every single battle, challenge, or obstacle you face. Amazingly, the same faith that is birthed in your heart at the new birth is what empowers you to win in the battles of life. Faith is your ultimate advantage!

FAITH MOVES EVERY MOUNTAIN

Our faith is the power that delivers our victories. Every battle is approached from the point of faith in God's power to win. Faith is the key to winning in every battle, challenge, or circumstance of life. Everything is possible by faith, and nothing is impossible to faith. Faith is a mountain-mover. Once faith is in place, every obstacle ceases to be a threat because faith has the capacity to remove every obstacle; be it a physical or a spiritual obstacle, as we would see in the following story:

A story is told of a girl who went hiking with her parents and on their way encountered a hill which kind of interrupted their journey. This girl wasn't pleased one bit about this seemingly innocent hill lying in the way of her fun. She then laid it to heart to pray to God to remove this hill off her way and was committed to praying over and again about it. It had become her own enemy of progress, so to say. Do you know what? It wasn't long until a government agency needed to construct a warehouse astound that axis. As a result, they had to remove that particular hill out of the way of their construction project. That was how a little girl's faith literally moved a hill.

I know exactly what you may be thinking; you may be saying, well, it is a mere coincidence. But you see, it might actually seem like a coincidence, but alas, it is not a coincidence. It was actually the little girl's faith that leveled the hill. And if you believe just like she did, your faith will move, not just a hill but a mountain.

Jesus, in teaching His disciples on the possibilities that lie with faith, said they could literally tell a mountain to go right into the sea if they had faith.

"For verily I say unto you, If ye have faith as a grain of mustard seed, ye shall say unto this mountain, Remove hence to yonder place, and it shall remove, and nothing shall be impossible unto you." Matthew 17:20

And I can assure you when Jesus made that statement, He was referring to a literal mountain. The word mountain can also be a metaphorical representation of the various problems and challenges of life. It could be a mountain of marital challenge, the mountain of financial problems, or debt; it could be a mountain of health issues like the woman with the issue of blood (Mark 5:25). However, it doesn't matter what mountain it is, you can eliminate it with the force of your faith. Be it sickness, disease, loss of job, money, a loved one, or any other challenging circumstance of life, faith is your victory. Your faith in God will cause an irreversible supernatural shift to your advantage. All you need to do is believe!

"Jesus saith unto her, Said I not unto thee, that, if thou wouldest believe, thou shouldest see the glory of God?" John 11:40

IT'S A NEW DAY FOR YOU

You are born a winner, not a loser. You are not to be defeated by anything visible or invisible. You are ordained to reign over obstacles and challenges. In other words, you can face giants, kick down walls and reach your goals. You can overcome sickness, diseases, and whip the devil out of his wits because you are not ordinary, but a champion. The moment you come to this realization; a new dawn will practically break forth for you.

As a champion, you have already defied the odds by surviving the most gruesome battle of them all—the race to the egg. Millions of sperms competed with you, but you won them all. And now that you are a giant, why do you even doubt victory against smaller numbers and wider margins? Why do you tremble at minor obstacles that cannot, in any way, be compared to what you have already overcome?

In fact, the only walls that exist are those you have placed in your minded life, And whatever obstacles you conceive, exist only because you have forgotten what you have already achieved. In other words, not only that you win at birth, but you also won at the new birth, victory is your new name. You can no longer be defeated!

If you are going to win in the battles of life, if you are going to thrive in difficult situations, you must see yourself from the eyes of God. You must believe all that Jesus died for on the cross of Calvary, and aggressively release your faith to see it practically manifest in your life. I tell you if you have the ever-winning faith if you will dare to believe, and act on your faith; it won't matter what circumstances or challenges you are faced with, you will come out a winner. Always remember, the greater one lives on the inside of you.

2

DEFEAT YOUR FEAR

To win in the battles of life, you must defeat fear. If you don't, it is very likely that your faith will not work. And that means you will be defeated. Fear and faith do not co-exist. Once fear walks in, faith walks out. The moment you allow fear to grip your heart, your faith is would be paralyzed. Hence, trying to exercise faith when you are afraid is an exercise in futility. The first battle you will have to fight for your faith to work is not a battle with the devil, it is not a battle with the circumstances; the battle you must fight and overcome will be the fight against fear.

Is it possible for a person who is born to win, to end up defeated? You may ask. The answer is a big YES! When you allow fear, doubt, unbelief to get into your heart, I tell you, it can paralyze you so much you may even begin to doubt the ability of your God.

WHAT FEAR REALLY IS

Fear is negative faith. Faith is confidence—in the ability of your enemy. Fear is believing the negative promise or threat of your enemy. It is believing the ability of the enemy over the ability of God. Every time you are afraid, you have lost touch with God's presence, and God's ability. Fear is not just a feeling of panic or trepidation, fear is a spirit, just like faith is a spirit (2 Corinthians 4:13).

"For God hath not given us the spirit of fear, but of power, and of love, and of a sound mind." 2 Timothy 1:7

Fear sponsors doubt and doubt sponsors defeat. If you are afraid, you will doubt as well. Fear is like a crippling paralysis that not only grips your heart but demobilizes your inner strength, resolves, and belief in God. Fear gives satan access into your life. It opens the door to the operations of darkness in your life.

Fear is putting idols above God Almighty. Fear is the result of ignorance, past negative experiences, or feeding the wrong diet. When the lion that should prey on sheep begins to feed on grass, it will lose sight of its identity and as a result, be threatened or even killed by the same things he should be feeding on. If you let fear into your heart, you will be a prey to your enemy!

THE SEAT OF YOUR FAITH

Your heart is the seat of your faith. It is with the heart that you believe in God. As you receive the word in your heart, faith is born in your heart.

"For with the heart man believeth unto righteousness,

and with the mouth, confession is made unto salvation." Romans 10:10

Not only that our heart plays a pivotal role in our salvation experience, but it also plays an important role in determining whether we win or lose in the battles of life. Our heart is the battlefield. Consequently, the real battles of life are not won on the battlefield with swords, chariots, or like in our day with armored tanks, AK-47 rifles, and grenades; the battles of life are won both in the heart and in the mind. This is how a professional athlete's coach described this inner struggle; "throw your mind over the bar, and your body will follow." This statement holds true, not only in the field of athletics but also in the battles of life.

You have to understand that winning is an inside thing. For as within, so without. When you win on the inside, it will simply manifest on the outside. It's just a matter of time. But if you allow fear to defeat you on the inside, then no miracle will save you from being defeated in the actual circumstances of life. Again, it's just a matter of time.

If we believe in our hearts that we will win in the battles of life, that would be the case. On the contrary, if fear and doubt take over our hearts, we may even be defeated long before the battle ever starts.

DEAD ON ARRIVAL

I heard about this particular story of how two men were conscripted into the army during a civil war in their nation. Before they were taken to the war front, they were both given the opportunity to say goodbye to their loved ones. The first man hugged his wife and with the last kiss whispered into her ear, "I shall be back!". The other said to his wife, "honey, kiss me goodbye because I don't know if I am going to make it." This he said with so much trepidation in his voice. Both men jumped into the army wagon along with other new conscripts.

While on the battlefield, the enemies attacked them from all fronts, leaving many soldiers severely wounded and scores dead. Amazingly, that recruit who told his wife he would be back received several bullets shots into his body, maybe twenty or more; but to the surprise of everyone, he survived and went back home to his wife. But the second soldier who was despondent and scared as to whether he would make it or not; got just one bullet shot on his ankle, and sadly he died instantly.

What exactly made the difference? Fear and faith. The first man had faith, the other was overtaken by fear. And true the usual wise saying, the coward among them died a thousand deaths before he really died. And I can tell you, it was not really the bullet that hit his ankle that killed him, it was his fear. It was the fear that had taken grip of his heart.

I realize there is a tendency to get afraid when we face the inevitable battles of life. However, you cannot afford to be afraid. If you do, not only that victory will elude you, you might actually end up being defeated. When we face trying times, difficult battles, and challenges of life, we have one of two hard choices to make, either we surrender our entire lives to be governed and influenced by fear or to take absolute charge of our life by faith in the revealed word of God.

WHEN THE WORSE HAPPENS

For instance, when you experience a turbulent time in your life, such as the loss of a loved one, the loss of a job, relationship, or when there is a negative medical diagnosis, or facing tough legal battles; the tendency is to panic and surrender to fear. And I can tell you, that is almost the easiest, thing to do; in fact, you don't even require any effort to travel that route. All you need to do is to give in. But you can decide to face your fears, defy all the odds against you and emerge as a winner. That will require faith in God. But much more than that, you will need to do something about your heart.

GUARD YOUR HEART

To avoid caving into fear in the middle of the challenging circumstances of life, we need to master how to guard our hearts. We need to protect it from external invasion as prescribed in the word of God.

"Keep thy heart with all diligence; for out of it are the issues of life." Proverbs 4:23

The Amplified Classic Version puts it this way:

"Keep and guard your heart with all vigilance and above all that you guard, for out of it flows the spirits of life." Proverbs 4:23 (AMPC).

Notice, the keyword here is the word "guard". In fact, in the above translation, it was mentioned twice for the sake of emphasis, indicating that it is very important. Guarding your heart is not only vital to keeping fear away, but it is also vital because to keep sickness away. If you can keep fear away from your heart, you can keep sickness and every other evil away from your life. If you can keep fear away, you can overcome any challenge that may come your way, no matter what it is.

But if you don't guard your heart, fear will find its way in, and take a hold of your heart. And when that happens, tragedy is inevitable! That will not be your story in Jesus' name!

The word, "keep" used in the King James Version is the Hebrew word, "nâtsar" usually pronounced, "naw-tsarr"', which means to guard, watch, watch over, preserve, to be blockaded, or to be a watchman. Actually, to keep or guard is a security word, which means to protect something valuable from external invaders. You know, invaders only go for treasures. If you have treasures, you have to pay the price for security. You have to buy it if need be. Otherwise, not only that you will lose valuable treasures, you will lose ground too.

Your heart is your greatest asset in the school of faith, and the devil knows that. That is why he keeps bombarding your minds with negativity. He is aware that whatever enters your mind will enter your heart and subsequently your life. So, if you carelessly let fear into your heart, you will lose your faith in God and hence your victory.

WATCH WHAT YOU WATCH

It takes real hard work to guard your mind. It is said that thousands of thoughts pass through our minds every second. Unfortunately, the majority of those thoughts are negative. So, if you are to stay positive in a negative world, or circumstances, it will be by the dint of hard work. Remember, the mind is the door to your heart, but the door to your mind are the five senses; the sense of sight, hearing, touch (feeling), smell, and taste. Whatever enters your mind will enter your heart, and whatever enters your heart will enter your life. It may not be visible immediately, but sooner than later, it will manifest itself in your life. To guard your heart will require that you take charge of all these faculties, especially the eyes, and the ear. I can tell you, this requires a lot of hard work on your part.

The question is, why is it so important for us to guard our hearts? The Bible tells us that out of it flows the issues of life. More so, because fear, like faith, comes from hearing. If fear enters your heart, it is only because you let it. You have the right and the ability to keep fear out of your life. And the key is, watch what you watch and hear. If you watch late nights horror movies and then go to bed afterward, you better not be shocked when you see strange creatures chasing you in the dreams. Now, this is not to say they only result from watching late-night movies, but that is what you are likely to get after watching such a movie at night.

On the other hand, if you feed your mind continuously on circular new media with its characteristic focus on "bad news", you will not have faith but fear. And this is without prejudice to all the circular media houses of our time. The point is, you cannot afford to allow every kind of junk to enter your mind and expect to walk in faith. You have to realize that fear, like faith, comes from hearing. In fact, even the word of God gains entrance into our hearts via the eye and the ear gates. But if we fail to take charge of our gates, we would probably be fired either accept defeat or denial the supremacy of fear over our lives.

DON'T LIVE IN DENIAL

Never live in denial of your feeling of fear. To deny the presence of fear is one of the greatest demonstrations of spiritual immaturity. That is deceiving yourself. Make no mistakes about it, faith is not the denial of the facts, but the acknowledgment and confidence that God can do what He promised to do, regardless of all the facts.

Choosing to acknowledge the reality of fear does not necessarily mean that you have surrendered to its power; it only shows that you are willing to deal with it. In fact, faith in itself is not merely false fearlessness, but intentional surrender to God's will, despite what we may feel. It is relying on the victory of Christ's cross rather than our strength. So, you don't need to deny you are afraid, instead, you are to deny fear the opportunity to exert its power over you. You are to confront and overcome it with the force of your faith. Remember, courage fueled by faith is not the absence of fear but the ability to withstand it, to face it, and above all to conquer it. Ultimately, if we are to develop this internal state of strength, we must take time to face our fears, redirect our focus, anchor our minds on the word of God, God's power. We must refuse to fear.

ANCHOR YOUR HEART ON THE WORD OF GOD

Just like faith, fear is also a powerful force. Its impact often pierces the deepest parts of us, quickly destabilizing our sense of safety, security, and state of calm. The truth is, we cannot escape the reality of fear in our world today. From the ongoing uncertainty of a global pandemic, the division of racial injustice, the fact that almost every nation is separated either on racial, political, religious, or ethnic grounds. This is not talking about the impact that all these are exerting on our emotional, psychological, spiritual, and physical wellbeing. However, even during such a difficult season on earth, we still find the word of God as encouraging as ever. It is as we anchor our hearts on the word that His peace comes in to create the right environment of faith in our hearts.

"Thou wilt keep him in perfect peace, whose mind is stayed on thee: because he trusteth in thee." Isaiah 26:3

One of the most vital keys to overcoming fear is to anchor our minds on the word of God. The issues of life come from the heart. You are what you think in your heart. Therefore, feeding your heart with winning thoughts will astronomically increase your chances to win in all the affairs of your life.

It doesn't matter the instability in the system of the crisis in your personal life, if you will anchor your mind on the word of the living God, your heart will be protected from fear, doubt, anxiety and I believe. If you want to rise above fear to the place of perpetual victory, you must take absolute responsibility for the state of your heart. You must renew your mind to embrace good news, rather than bad news.

FOCUS ON GOD'S POWER

You can choose to focus on God and his power to fulfill

his promises. Your focus determines the direction of your life. You are either focusing on God and His power or on the storms of life. Once you take your eyes off God, fear will possess your heart. Remember Peter's experience walking on the water (Mark 4:35-41). As long as His focus was on Jesus, he was walking on water, but the moment he shifted his focus off Jesus to the direction of the storm, he instantly started drowning. Walking on water is a typical walk of faith. It is the picture of living the ever-winning life—a life of total victory over the storms or battles of life.

Circumstances of life may be difficult and force us to feel anxiety or to be afraid. Even so, we have a choice to rest in God's person, power, and provision instead of focusing on the storms that life brings our way. For instance, David did not focus on the size of Goliath but on the size of his God. He focuses on God's ability to keep his promises. And the result was a total victory (1 Samuel 17).

CAST YOUR CARES ON GOD

If you lose sight of God's ability, you will give room to anxiety, doubt, leading to fear. Nevertheless, we can choose to cast all our care upon our Lord and Savior, Jesus Christ just like Peter admonished:

"Humble yourselves, therefore, under the mighty hand of God so that at the proper time he may exalt you, casting all your anxieties on him, because he cares for you,

Be sober-minded; be watchful. Your adversary the devil prowls around like a roaring lion, seeking someone to devour. Resist him, firm in your faith, knowing that the same kinds of suffering are being experienced by your brotherhood throughout the world." 1 Peter 5:6-9

The original Greek definition for the word humble is to dismiss self-reliance and become fully dependent on God. How easy it is to attempt to face fear in our strength. The result of such efforts often increases our discouragement and prolongs our worry over what we cannot change.

But as we learn to acknowledge our limitations and need for God's authority over our lives, we are enabled to rest in our dependency and trust in His sovereignty. In doing so, we are more open to bringing our anxiety to the Lord and casting those burdens onto the One who strengthens us.

REFUSE TO FEAR

You must be like David who refused to fear. The Psalmist David understood what it means to rise above fear. He did not deny the fact that he was threatened by the negative prevailing circumstances of his day. Yet in spite of all the troubles and battles surrounding his life, he refused to fear. He locked his heart against fear.

"The Lord is my light and my salvation; whom shall I fear? the Lord is the strength of my life; of whom shall I be afraid? When the wicked, even mine enemies and my foes, came upon me to eat up my flesh, they stumbled and fell. Though a host should encamp against me, my heart shall not fear: though war should rise against me, in this will I be confident." Psalm 27:1-5

"God is our refuge and strength, a very present help in trouble. Therefore, will not we fear, though the earth is removed, and though the mountains are carried into the midst of the sea; Though the waters thereof roar and be troubled, though the mountains shake with the swelling thereof. Selah." Psalm 46:1-3

We live in a world and time where fear is normal, and where everyone wants to be politically correct. So, when you decide to rise above the negativity around you, you will be seen as either a weirdo or an insensitive or impractical fellow. But if you really want to have victory and win in all areas of life, then you must hold into your faith.

Ultimately, defeating fear is a milestone effort in the school of faith.

3

SPEAK TO THE
MOUNTAIN

The ever-winning faith is a speaking faith. It is faith that not only believes but boldly declares what it believes. Belief in God is not a passive concept, but an absolutely active reality that is boldly expressed in words. One of the surest pieces of proof that a person believes in the power of God is through their words. As a matter of fact, anything too big for your mouth is too big for your life.

Remember the story of the fig tree. It was the next morning after the triumphant entry of Jesus into Jerusalem. Having spent the night at Bethany, along with His disciples, he was now hungry and needed something to eat. He see this fig tree before him and walked up to it expecting to find fruits to satisfy his hunger. Unfortunately, He found no fruits on it, and of course, we are told that it was not the time of the figs. In other words, it was not its season of producing fruits. But then Jesus cursed the tree. He spoke to it. Of course, we are told that "his disciples heard it." So, he was audible enough to be heard.

"And on the morrow, when they came from Bethany, he was hungry: And seeing a fig tree afar off having leaves, he came, if haply he might find anything thereon: and when he came to it, he found nothing but leaves; for the time of figs was not yet. And Jesus answered and said unto it, No man eat the fruit of thee hereafter forever. And his disciples heard it." Mark 1:12-14

And as if nothing happened, they continued their journey. It was not until the next day, while they were passing by that Peter, one of Jesus' disciples noticed that the fig tree had dried up. And so, he was curious and called Jesus' attention to what He had noticed. It was at that point that Jesus, in his usual manner unveiled one of the biggest lessons on the subject of faith—speaking to the mountain.

"And in the morning, as they passed by, they saw the fig tree dried up from the roots. And Peter calling to remembrance saith unto him, Master, behold the fig tree which thou cursedst is withered away. And Jesus answering saith unto them, Have faith in God. For verily I say unto you, That whosoever shall say unto this mountain, Be thou removed, and be thou cast into the sea; and shall not doubt in his heart, but shall believe that those things which he saith shall come to pass; he shall have whatsoever he saith." Mark 11:20-24

SPEAKING BOLDLY

The lesson of the fig tree is a classic example of how

faith operates. It believes, then it SPEAKS. It addresses the mountain boldly. And with that, Jesus literally gave his disciples, and to you and me the inside scoop on how to deal with mountains—the challenges and battles of life. He says we are to speak to it. You don't negotiate with your mountains, you don't cry about the mountain, you don't beg your mountain, you simply tell it what to do. There is a place to pray to God, but there is a place for speaking directly to your challenges, or obstacles. If you truly have faith, it will show up through your vocal cords. Jesus did not negotiate with the fig tree, he spoke to it. He did not negotiate or pray to God about the storm He and His disciples were in (Mark 4), He simply spoke boldly to it.

In the acts of the Apostle, the Bible talks about speaking boldly in the Lord.

"Long time, therefore, abode they speaking boldly in the Lord, which gave testimony unto the word of his grace, and granted signs and wonders to be done by their hands." Acts 14:3

One of the keys to signs and wonder, the key to experiencing the power of God like never before, be it in your life, your family, health or business is to speak boldly in the Lord. And like Jesus, when you find yourself in a storm, threatening to capsize the boat of your life, when you see the devil trying to mess with health, your family, your little ones; when it seems like your business is about to cave in, or when some fellow threatens to destroy your life with that lawsuit; come on, you don't need to cry, you don't need to beg, you don't need to negotiate with the mountain; what you need to do is to speak to it.

Remember, you are a king (Revelations 6:10), and Kings don't beg. Kings don't beg issues, kings issue decrees. When kings speak, everyone stands at attention. The words of a king command obedient compliance, and their words are with authority backed with power. They don't engage in arguments.

"Where the word of a king is, there is power: and who may say unto him, What doest thou?" Ecclesiastes 8:4

"Thou shalt also decree a thing, and it shall be established unto thee: and the light shall shine upon thy ways." Job 22:28

And as a person of faith, you are not to beg issues, you are to be in command of issue. You are to speak to your battles, speak to the devil, and the challenges with all the balls you have got. You know, before God, you can afford to be gentle, and express your love and reverence for Him, but before the devil or a stubborn challenge in your life; you will have to aggressively address it and tell it where to go. That is what faith is about.

SOMETHING TO SHOUT ABOUT

And I can assure you, there is power in your words. There

is power in your words to literally transform the prevailing circumstances of your existence. That is what speaking to your mountain is all about. Nothing is as powerful as words.

"A man's belly shall be satisfied with the fruit of his mouth; and with the increase of his lips shall he be filled. Death and life are in the power of the tongue: and they that love it shall eat the fruit thereof." Proverbs 18:20-21.

Your words are either empowering you or weakening you. Your life right now is a direct testament to the words you have been speaking all along. If you are hungry, it's your words, if you are satisfied, it's your words. Whether you make it in life or not depends a lot on how you use your words. It was the negative mindset expressed through negative words that left a negative verdict on Israelites while on their way to the promised land. In fact, their words stopped them from entering their promise.

"Say unto them, As truly as I live, saith the Lord, as ye have spoken in mine ears, so will I do to you: Your carcasses shall fall in this wilderness; and all that were numbered of you, according to your whole number, from twenty years old and upward, which have murmured against me, Doubtless ye shall not come into the land, concerning which I sware to make you dwell therein, save Caleb the son of Jephunneh, and Joshua the son of Nun. But your little ones, which ye said should be a prey, they will I bring

in, and they shall know the land which ye have despised."
Numbers 14:28-31

Negative words will ultimately drown those speaking
them. It doesn't matter their current condition. On the
other hand, those who continuously say nothing will
consistently see nothing. It is not enough to have faith,
it has to be released through words to produce results.
These are often referred to as faith declarations. But is
much more than that, it is speaking to your mountain.
I tell you, this is one of the most important aspects of
faith. In fact, your faith will always rise to the level of your
declarations, and your bold declarations are what will give
you possession of what you say. Surprisingly, God's word
in your mouth is as powerful as God's word in His mouth.

YOU HAVE THE SPIRIT OF FAITH

The God-kind of faith is not just a belief in the word of
God, it is a spirit. And the spirit of faith is a talking spirit.
When you truly believe, you are compelled to speak in
accordance with what you believe. If you believe you are
healed as the word of God rightly says, you will command
the sickness to go away and health to be restored back to
you. That is how the spirit of faith manifests.

"We having the same spirit of faith, according to as it is
written, I believed, and therefore have I spoken; we also
believe, and therefore speak." 2 Corinthians 4:13

The spirit of faith does not command results by keeping mute; it commands results by boldly declaring the word. Anything too big for your mouth is too big for your life. It is what you declare boldly that God will confirm. If you cannot boldly command things to change, then you don't deserve it.

WHEN YOU SPEAK, YOU CREATE IT

The creative power of faith is released as we speak. When you declare a thing, you bring it into being. Even if it did not exist before, your words can create it much like God created the universe in the first chapter of Genesis. Words are creative. The Bible talks about God creating the fruits of the lips.

"I create the fruit of the lips; Peace, peace to him that is far off, and to him that is near, saith the Lord, and I will heal him." Isaiah 57:19

The word of God spoken by the lips of faith has the capacity to move the mountain and resolve any issue in your life, whatever it is. The most powerful creative raw material for creating all possibilities is the spoken word. The world was not only created by words, it is also held together and governed by words.

"Through faith, we understand that the worlds were framed by the word of God so that things which are seen were not made of things which do appear." Hebrews 11:3

"In the beginning, God created heaven and the earth. And the earth was without form, and void, and darkness was upon the face of the deep. And the Spirit of God moved upon the face of the waters. And God said, Let there be light: and there was light." Genesis 1:1

"In the beginning was the Word, and the Word was with God, and the Word was God. The same was at the beginning with God. All things were made by Him, and without Him was not anything made that was made." John 1:1-3

"Who being the brightness of His glory, and the express image of His person, and upholding all things by the word of His power..." Hebrews 1:3

WHEN YOU SPEAK, YOU COMMIT GOD

God is absolutely committed to His word, but until you speak it, power is never released to bring it to pass. The Bible says he will hasten His words to perform it. Remember the centurion whose servant was ill, but as Jesus attempted to follow him to heal her, the faith-filled man said there was no need. He said should speak the word only and his servant will be healed.

"And Jesus saith unto him, I will come and heal him. The centurion answered and said, Lord, I am not worthy that thou shouldest come under my roof: but speak the word only, and my servant shall be healed. For I am a man under authority, having soldiers under me: and I say to this man, Go, and he goeth; and to another, Come, and he cometh; and to my servant, Do this, and he doeth it." Matthew 8:7-9

Jesus was definitely amazed at his faith. The Bible tells us that his servant was healed that same hour. That is the power of words.

That terminal disease will not move by wishing or crying, it will move by commanding. If you have faith, you will say to this mountain. It's time to rise up with boldness and speak to that mountain of sickness, cancer,....speak to it against all odds, speak to that dying business, command it to come alive. Speak to that... Come and the work of your hand to prosper.

You may say, "well, you know sometimes, these things are easier said than done." Especially when you have the obvious facts before you. Imagine you have this negative medical diagnosis, and you are there feeling spirit for yourself wondering what to do next. But well, even in difficult times like that, the power of words still holds true; and if will engage with it, you will experience a turnaround. Although it may appear difficult, that is exactly why you need to do it by faith. Try to speak despite the obvious symptoms you may be having, or the negative impact of the crisis. Release your faith by the word of command. Remember, you have what you say.

WHEN YOU SPEAK, ANGELS MOVE!

Words are very important to activate angels. And when it comes to answered prayer, you are looking at the ministry of Angel. It is our words that put angels to work. They are our God-ordained ministers sent by God to minister for us. "Are they not all ministering spirits, sent forth to minister for them who shall be heirs of salvation?" Hebrews 1:14. That means they are always waiting on us to issue the instructions in the name of Jesus. When an angel came to Daniel, he acknowledged that he was sent on account of Daniel's words.

"Then said he unto me, Fear not, Daniel: for from the first day that you did set your heart to understand, and to chasten yourself before your God, your words were heard, and I am come for thy words. Daniel 10:12

Although Angels are very powerful, when we issue instructions in the name of Jesus, they obey us; because they are designed to respond to our words.

"Bless the Lord, ye his angels, that excel in strength, that do his commandments, hearkening unto the voice of his word." Psalm 103:20

When you speak, when you issue commands, they are the ones responsible for carrying it out. But it must be voiced. That means you have to issue the command.

A young lady in Africa traveled home from the city, but

while driving back on the highway, she suddenly noticed two hard racing behind her. After observing carefully from her side mirrors, she decided to increase the speed. On doing that, those two SUVs seemed to increase their speed too. Oh, your guess is as good as hers, they were armed robbers or probably assassins. And by this time, they were apparently closing in on her. By this time, she knew she had to do something. Then she remembered the ministry of angels. So, she suddenly screened at the top of her voice, "angels of God, puncture their four tires!" It wasn't even up to a second after she gave that command when the four tires of the two SUVs busted simultaneously, and the two vehicles somersaulted into the air right behind her, while she drove away. It was so dramatic that she was shocked herself. That is how to provoke the ministry of angels—through words.

Until you speak, nothing will change. Everything moves in response to your words. Take for instance a father and a child. Instructions are only carried out when you voice them out. You can't wish a child to do something, and actually expect him/her to do it. You will have to tell him what you want him/her to do, right? Also, our most important means of communication are our words. And that is how we get to deploy Angels—through our words.

WHEN YOU SPEAK, MOUNTAINS MOVE

Once you have a working revelation of what God has

made available, and your convictions are intact, the next thing is to speak. The reason many people's hopes and are dashed is that a lot of people try to address everything to God. There are situations where you speak to God about problems, but if you want to see maximum results, you must learn how to speak to your mountain. Jesus gave us the assurance that if we would speak to the mountain, it will be moved.

Your faith will move mountains if you are willing to speak to the mountain. When you understand the place of your spoken word in the overall dynamics of faith, it will position you to rule over every battle or negative circumstances that will come your way. Jesus spoke to the fig tree to show teach us how faith operates, faith will amount to nothing until is it released by speaking. Everything was created by words, and they are still controlled by the spoken word. I tell you, no matter how stubborn your problems are, they will bow to the dominating power of the spoken word. I mean, it will literally get out of your way.

Faith is absolute present tense confidence in the word of God. If you truly believe in the ability and integrity of God to perform his word you will declare that word with audacity. You will speak to your mountain!

4

THE BATTLE IS THE LORD'S

As a believer, you are constantly in a battle with an enemy ready to take you out at the slightest opportunity. If you can be honest with yourself, you will agree with me that we are always in one battle or another. If it is not in health, it's in your finances, career, marriage, or even with your kids. At other times, it could be battles in the area of relationships, including fathers and their children, and between neighbors.

The good news is that as God's covenant children, God himself is committed to fighting for all is. When we face difficult life challenges, we must take solace in the fact that God's power is always available to help us through it all. God is not only aware of the battles we each face in the course of our lives, He is ever ready to support us till we gain full victory over the enemy.

RELY TOTALLY ON HIM

For God to fight for you, you must come to a point of absolute dependence on Him. Never go into any battle thinking you can do it on your own. No, you can't! You cannot run the race of the spirit in the energy of the flesh. If you attempt it, you will not only be defeated, you might even lose your life in the process. One of your greatest assets in times of battles or crises is your dependence on God.

Unfortunately, some people would want to rely on their own energy to their peril. But for the believer, it is not so. We must learn to trust God for our victory over the enemy.

"Some trust in chariots, and some in horses: but we will remember the name of the Lord our God." Psalm 20:7

"Woe to them that go down to Egypt for help; and stay on horses, and trust in chariots, because they are many; and in horsemen, because they are very strong; but they look not unto the Holy One of Israel, neither seek the Lord!" Isaiah 31:1

If you ever want to have victory over the enemy, if you want to win the battles of life, NEVER rely on your power; instead, always rely on the power of the Almighty. In fact, even in situations where you actually have everything figured out; you still have to keep your trust in God. This does not in any way negate the need for thorough preparation; even after quality preparation, you must rely on God for his grace.

"The horse is prepared against the day of battle: but safety is of the Lord." Proverbs 21:31

We are in conflict with demonic forces that are capable of wreaking havoc on our lives, marriage, business, health, etc. So, naturally speaking, we are no match for these evil forces. One demon can actually decimate thousands of people at the same time. Remember the seven sons of Sceva, who went to cast out a devil in the name of Jesus; it took just one demon to mesmerize them. In fact, their clothes were torn to shreds by this one demon-possessed individual.

"And there were seven sons of one Sceva, a Jew, and chief of the priests, which did so. And the evil spirit answered and said, Jesus I know, and Paul I know; but who are ye? And the man in whom the evil spirit was leaped on them, and overcame them, and prevailed against them, so that they fled out of that house naked and wounded." Acts 19:14-16

So, on our own, we cannot match them. That is the reason we cannot attempt to fight on our own. But we can choose to rely on the power of the Holy Spirit.

"Then he answered and spake unto me, saying, This is the word of the Lord unto Zerubbabel, saying, Not by might, nor by power, but by my spirit, saith the Lord of hosts." Zechariah 4:6

FACING YOUR GIANTS

That was the case with David. The story of David and Goliath clearly shows how God fights for His people. David was only a shepherd boy and the youngest of the eight sons of Jesse of who was a Bethlehemite. It happened that King Saul and his army were all on the battlefield. Goliath, the giant of the Philistines, threw a challenge to the army of Israel. Unfortunately, the men of Saul's army were afraid of Goliath, and there was no one to stand up to him.

When David got to the battlefield to bring supplies to his older brothers, he was embarrassed to see Goliath defying the army of God. David, filled with faith and a passion for God's name which was being blasphemed by Goliath, took Goliath's challenge. His faith was so strong that he was willing to face Goliath, knowing that God would help him defeat Goliath. David understood how to turn the battle over to God. Notice, David was not moved by the size of Goliath, though intimidating, instead, he looked to the size of his God. He focused on the power of God available to him. In other words, the "giants" or battles, we face are never the real problem, it is our lack of faith that is our greatest undoing. But I can tell you when faith arises in you, giants fall.

"Then said David to the Philistine, Thou comest to me with a sword, and with a spear, and with a shield: but I come to thee in the name of the Lord of hosts, the God of the armies of Israel, whom thou hast defied. This day will the Lord deliver thee into mine hand; and I will smite thee, and take thine head from thee; and I will give the carcases of the host of the Philistines this day unto the fowls of the air, and to the wild beasts of the earth; that all the earth may know that there is a God in Israel."1 Samuel 17: 45-47

It happened that when he took steps against Goliath, God honored his steps of faith with a supernatural victory. He literally cut off the head of Goliath.

"So David prevailed over the Philistine with a sling and with a stone, and smote the Philistine, and slew him; but there was no sword in the hand of David. Therefore, David ran, and stood upon the Philistine, and took his sword, and drew it out of the sheath thereof, and slew him, and cut off his head therewith. And when the Philistines saw their champion was dead, they fled." 1 Samuel 17:50-51

The story of David and Goliath is just one of the many accounts written for us, to encourage us to trust in God even in the midst of the greatest of challenges. Another vital lesson we can learn is that the God we serve is capable of defeating any of the giants in our lives. Be it fear, poverty, depression, financial issues, ill health, marital challenges, or whatever else it may be. If we know Him and His nature well enough to step out in faith, we will be like David—a winner! That means, even when we are not sure what tomorrow would bring, we have to trust Him all the way.

LET GOD FIGHT YOUR BATTLES

Like David, you are not to run from your enemies. If you run from your enemies—from your battles—you will have to live with them thereafter. You know a lot of challenges never go away unless you are willing to confront them. God wants you to face your enemies while trusting him to deliver you from them. However, when you choose to trust him, He'll fight for you. Of course, He is definitely going to win the battle for you.

"The Lord shall fight for you and you shall hold your peace." Exodus 14: 14

But the problem is usually with us. Sometimes, we are trying to rely on our strength, at other times, we are just not patient enough to allow the Lord to fight on our behalf. We feel the Lord is too slow in reacting and would rather fight ourselves. Especially when the battle seems urgent and threatening. We can still trust God.

When the people of Israel faced a threatening battle with the children of Moab and Ammon, God's word to them is a major encouragement to everyone facing the battles of life:

"Do not be afraid or discouraged because of this vast army. For the battle is not yours, but God's." 2 Chronicles 20:15 (NIV)

God is always there to stand and fight for us through the battles of life. But for that to happen, we have to be yielded, we have to be willing to receive God's help.

GET OUT OF GOD'S WAY

When attempting to save someone who is drowning, you cannot save them as long as they are trying to do it for themselves. Of course, we can understand the person's survival instinct trying to manifest itself in such danger. But if the rescue process is to succeed at all, they must let go of their own effort to save themselves and rely on the person trying to save them. The danger of trying to save or rescue a drowning man is that the person can pull you down. So, what you need to do is to keep treading water until they actually give up trying on their own. At that point, the rescue process becomes very easy. All you will need to do is simply place your hand on their shoulder and swim back to safety.

That is exactly how it works in our relationship with God. As long as we are trying to fight the battles of life in our own strength, we are probably going to hit the rocks, we are going to drown. But as soon as we yield to God's help in the battle, our enemies will be defeated.

When the people of Israel faced such a threat, the first thing they did was to gather to pray and ask God for help.

"O our God, wilt thou not judge them? for we have no might against this great company that cometh against us; neither know we what to do: but our eyes are upon thee." 2 Chronicles 20:12

Notice what they said, "we have no might of our own..." Now, here is how God's Word Translation (GWT) puts it:

"We don't have the strength to face this large crowd that is attacking us..."

For God to step on the scene and fight your enemies, you must first and foremost acknowledge that you cannot fight the battle on your own. It is your reliance on Him that brings His power to work on your behalf. And the way to get God on your side is to go to him in prayer. Every time, we ask God for His help in battle, our enemies are decimated.

"When I cry unto thee, then shall mine enemies turn back: this I know; for God is for me." Psalm 56:9

Depending on God does not mean that you lack God's power in your life, it only indicates that you know when to hand over your battles to Him, realizing that there are battles only God can fight. In other words, when you feel powerless against the enemy, that is a perfect time to step back and let God fight for you. Remember, He has all the power to fight for you.

"God hath spoken once; twice have I heard this; that power belongeth unto God." Psalm 62:11. Jesus said that all power in heaven and in the earth has been given unto him (Matthew 28:18). And since God is a man of war (Exodus 15:3), then you might as well rely on Him to fight your battles.

ENGAGE DIVINE STRATEGY

However, you must find out His strategy. You know, everything bows to strategy. There is a divine strategy for every battle. If you want God to fight for you, you must be ready to let God have His way; you must be patient enough to discern God's strategy. Remember, God's ways are always higher than our ways. It is possible that God wants you to do it in a particular way. Amazingly! God's strategies are usually unconventional.

After they had followed God's strategy and defeated their enemies, the army of Israel learned a major lesson. Just imagine, three well-trained armies were getting ready to fight with them. It is obvious that they outnumbered the army of Israel. But instead of giving in to fear, the army of Israel followed God's strategy. King Jehoshaphat was instructed to position singers before the fighters. That means, to prioritize worship over warfare. Amazingly, when they ascended in worship, the power of God descended in warfare against their enemies.

So a strategy that didn't make any sense became the secret to their victory. In fact, it was the enemies that destroyed themselves. What they used was the weapon of praise. It took praise (music), to provoke God to fight for them.

"Jehoshaphat stood and said, "Listen to me, O Judah and inhabitants of Jerusalem! Believe in the Lord your God and you will be established; believe his prophets." When he had taken counsel with the people, he appointed those who were to sing to the Lord and praise him in holy splendor, as they went before the army, saying, "Give thanks to the Lord, for his steadfast love endures forever. "As they began to sing and praise, the Lord set an ambush against the Ammonites, Moab, and Mount Seir, who had come against Judah, so that they were routed. For the Ammonites and Moab attacked the inhabitants of Mount Seir, destroying them utterly; and when they had made an end of the inhabitants of Seir, they all helped to destroy one another." 2 Chronicles 20:20-23

They did not only defeat their enemies, but they also had a vast collection of spoils of war. In fact, it took 3 days to collect all the spoils of war. If you are able to discern God's strategy, you are well on your way to victory. Remember, God's own strategy never fails.

In the case of Jericho wall, God's strategy was to match around the city seven times, once every day, and 7 times on the 7th day, and blow the trumpet.

"And ye shall compass the city, all ye men of war, and go round about the city once. Thus shalt thou do six days. And seven priests shall bear before the ark seven trumpets of rams' horns: and the seventh day ye shall compass the city seven times, and the priests shall blow with the trumpets. And it shall come to pass, that when they make a long blast with the ram's horn, and when ye hear the sound of the trumpet, all the people shall shout with a great shout; and the wall of the city shall fall down flat, and the people shall ascend up every man straight before him." Joshua 6:3-5

That was strange, right? Of course, it didn't make sense at the time; but that was how they got their victory.

ENGAGE THE WEAPON OF FAITH

We live in an embattled world—a world full of oppositions on all sides. The amazing thing is that most of our challenges in life are more than what we have the capacity to handle and there is no human capacity that can resist them except through the fight of faith. Faith is the ultimate covenant force that destroys every barrier, enemy, and helps us to win in every battle that may come our way. So, whenever you find yourself in the midst of battles, remember the weapon of faith. God is always ready to help, if only we can trust him. The Bible states that the weapons of our warfare are not carnal (2 Corinthians 10:4).

Faith is our most proven weapon for conquest in the battle of life. Until we engage it, we can't become winners. No wonder the Bible says, "Above all, taking the shield of faith, wherewith ye shall be able to quench all the fiery darts of the wicked one" (Ephesians 6:16). This shows that faith is for fighting and not merely for making confessions as many Christians do. Remember, the Bible tells us to fight the good fight of faith (1 Timothy 6:12). As a matter of fact, faith is a major element in the whole armor of God that we can engage in fighting the battles of life. But no matter how hard the battle maybe, if we engage in a fight of faith, we are sure to win. If you are afflicted with sickness and you just wait or sit there believing God for healing, it will kill you, with God watching, because things never happen by waiting, they happen by acting. It is time to fight the fight of faith to win the battles of life!

HE CAME THROUGH FOR ME

If you trust him, he will come through for you. And I can personally tell you that while in a life-threatening situation in the then war-torn country of Liberia (in Africa), God proved himself, and I am excited to share a little bit of that experience with you:

Back in February of 1990, I traveled to Liberia as a missionary under the ministry I was in then: "The World

Soul Winning Evangelistic Ministry ". I was sent to pastor a church and evangelize the city. The church I pastored was Christ Apostolic Church located at Carey Street behind the Federal Post Office in Monrovia, Libera. I never knew there was a civil war going on in Liberia at that time until I got there.

Although the war had not entered the Monrovia city, which was the Federal Capital City where I was at the time; but by May 1990, the Rebel troops, (The Charles Taylor's troop and Prince Johnson's troop) had gained access to the Monrovia City; and the tension was very high. In fact, almost everyone was in a panic, wanting to get out of the bloody war.

While all that was going on, I got a phone call from the head office that sent me on that missionary assignment, asking to know my situation. They wanted to know if it would be possible for me to return to my home country, Nigeria. But the first question that struck my mind was, "who would take care of the people after the war?" And so, I thought to myself, "could this be the reason I was there in the first place? I had to decline the offer. I told the head office that I would volunteer myself to stay behind and take care of the needy people after the war.

That was exactly what I did, and I have no regrets. Now for want of space, I would not be able to give every detail of what I went through by that singular decision to stay back; but I must confess, it was a very gruesome experience of my lifetime. Thousands of people were massacred in that war. However, even while in that situation, I had my confidence in God. I didn't see myself dying in Liberia. And today, I can honestly tell you that through it all, God proved himself faithful. I mean, he literally came through for me; and I sincerely give him all the glory.

When God is set to help you, when He is set to fight for you, there are no barriers. There is no battle or barrier that can stop or defeat a man who has put his entire trust on God. As long as your trust is not in your ability, God will definitely fight for you. The Bible says, "Through You we will push down our enemies; Through Your name we will trample those who rise up against us. For I will not trust in my bow, Nor shall my sword save me. But You have saved us from our enemies, And have put to shame those who hated us." Psalm 44:5-7.

If we are going to win in these spiritual battles that we are constantly faced with, we must each trust God to fight for us. The reason I shared this story is to let you know that if you can just put your trust in God, you will not be disappointed. If He came through for me, He will come through for you!

5

THE POWER OF TESTIMONIES

There is absolutely nothing nearly as powerful and as effective in provoking faith as a living testimony of the gospel of our Lord Jesus Christ. The testimony of a miracle is a testament to the efficacy of the word, as well as the faithfulness of God. Jesus and His disciples used testimonies to confirm that the words that they spoke were the truth. It is one thing to know that the word of God is powerful, but it is another thing to see it practically manifest in peoples' lives.

People may argue about doctrine or the interpretation of Scripture, but no one can argue with a miracle. One testimony of a miracle of healing, deliverance, or breakthrough is far more effective than a thousand sermons. Miracles prove that Jesus is alive, they give witness to His resurrection. Without miracles, signs, and wonders, the resurrection would only sound like a mere theory to a lot of people. Testimonies are the vehicle for communicating these miracles.

"To whom also he showed himself alive after his passion by many infallible proofs, being seen of them forty days, and speaking of the things pertaining to the kingdom of God."

Jesus promised that as we preach the gospel, He will confirm the word we preach with signs and wonders.

"And these signs shall follow them that believe; In my name shall they cast out devils; they shall speak with new tongues; They shall take up serpents; and if they drink any deadly thing, it shall not hurt them; they shall lay hands on the sick, and they shall recover." Mark 16:17-18

Of course, when you study the Bible, you will see that when His disciples actually went out in obedience to that instruction, it was followed with signs and wonders.

"And they went forth and preached everywhere, the Lord working with them, and confirming the word with signs following. Amen."

And for all those who care to obey the same instructions of Jesus in our day, miracles, signs, and wonders also follow them, confirming the word, and proving the faithfulness. In fact, those who experience these miracles are living, walking proofs of God's power to fulfill what He promised.

I TESTIFY

To testify is to show that something is true or real, to give or provide proof of something. It means to make a statement based on personal knowledge, experience, or belief. It is to bear witness. To testify also refers to the act of expressing one's personal conviction. Testimonies of miracles and divine interventions serve as points of contact to bring people to a place of faith in God, thereby drafting multitudes into the kingdom of God. It is to declare openly what God has done for you. The blind man whose sight was restored by Jesus said, "one thing I know, that, whereas I was blind, now I see." In other words, testimony is a statement about an experience with God.

IT'S A FAITH BOOSTER

If you want to see your faith soar like never before, you need to engage the power of testimonies. One very powerful thing about testimonies is that they inspire your faith. Testimonies are like boosters or catalysts with the capacity to increase your faith. The principle behind testimonies is inherent in the fact that the God who helped others conquer their mountains is also able to help you conquer yours.

This is also called the law of precedence. It states that if it has been done for someone before, it can be done for you as well. The Bible teaches us that there is no respect for persons with God.

"Then Peter opened his mouth, and said, Of a truth, I perceive that God is no respecter of persons: But in every nation, he that feareth him, and worketh righteousness, is accepted with him." Acts 10:34

The point is, if God can do it for one person, He can and will do it for you if you meet the same conditions. Remember, God does not change. His nature and character do not change. He is like the North Star, constant any day, any time.

"For I am the Lord, I change not; therefore, ye sons of Jacob are not consumed." Malachi 3:6

"Jesus Christ the same yesterday, and today, and forever." Hebrews 13:8

Because of God's unchanging nature, we can trust him not just to do what He says, but to do for us the same things He did for someone else.

In the same vein, the God who helped you defeat your enemies in time past is still available to help you through your present challenges. In other words, if you can remember how He saved you in the past, you can activate within you an ever-winning faith. The truth is, you are here today simply because of the battles you have won in the past. I mean, the victories God has given you.

ON THE WINGS OF TESTIMONIES

This was one of the secrets of David's magnificent victory over Goliath. David rode on the wings of his past victories to defeat the champion of the Philistines. When David faced Goliath, he believed he would defeat Goliath. And I can tell you, one of the pillars upon which his faith stood was his experience with God. It was his testimonies of facing and killing the lion and the bear with the help of God. David was absolutely convinced of his victory before he took the first step. He figured that the same God who helped him kill the lion and the bear is also capable and faithful to delivering Goliath into his hands.

"And David said unto Saul, thy servant kept his father's sheep, and there came a lion, and a bear, and took a lamb out of the flock: And I went out after him, and smote him, and delivered it out of his mouth: and when he arose against me, I caught him by his beard, and smote him, and slew him. Thy servant slew both the lion and the bear: and this uncircumcised Philistine shall be as one of them, seeing he hath defied the armies of the living God." 1 Samuel 17:34-36

Once he caught a glimpse of that, his faith rushed like adrenaline. In fact, as Goliath was still trying to attack him, David courageously ran towards him, and with the help of God, David killed Goliath just like the lion and the bear. What bravery! What faith!

"And it came to pass, when the Philistine arose, and came and drew nigh to meet David, that David hasted, and ran toward the army to meet the Philistine. And David put his hand in his bag, and took thence a stone, and slang it, and smote the Philistine in his forehead, that the stone sunk into his forehead; and he fell upon his face to the earth. So David prevailed over the Philistine with a sling and with a stone, and smote the Philistine, and slew him, but there was no sword in the hand of David." 1 Samuel 17:48-50

REPLICATING DIVINE EXPERIENCES

The testimony of a miracle is the technology for replicating itself. Every testimony has in them the potential to multiply itself. When we share our testimonies (or good reports) of our faith, it helps others going through a similar challenge, not only to relate with our miracle but to trust God for their own miracle. And once they are able to trust God, the same miracle happens in their life. That is how testimonies replicate themselves. This is why it is critically important that we share our testimonies. Testimonies should not only be celebrated, they should be well-captured and shared. Thank God, we are blessed today to have the technology to do so. When we share our testimonies—of God's goodness in our lives, we multiply it. In other words, we make it possible for others to experience the same miracles in their own lives.

THE WOMAN WITH THE ISSUE OF BLOOD

It was testimonies that inspired the woman with the issue of blood to go after her miracle, against all odds. Having been ill for twelve solid years coupled with spending all her fortune on physicians, she must have come to the point where she was wary of people's suggestions. A lot of people would have suggested one solution or another. Unfortunately, none of them helped. Otherwise, we probably won't be reading her story today. Nevertheless, she didn't give up her search for answers, until the day she heard about Jesus. She heard of how Jesus healed every sick person who came in contact with Him. Of course, she must have probably heard of how He raised the dead, cleanse the lepper, open blind eyes, and how he vindicated a woman caught in the very act. Her perception of Him must have been that of a loving man. She could have figured that if Jesus could heal all these people, raise the dead, including forgiving the woman caught in adultery; then her own case is nothing compared. The good part was that the more she heard, the more her faith was built up until she finally decided to schedule her miracle.

"And a certain woman, which had an issue of blood twelve years, And had suffered many things of many physicians, and had spent all that she had, and was nothing bettered, but rather grew worse, When she had heard of Jesus, came in the press behind, and touched his garment. For she said If I may touch but his clothes, I shall be whole. And

71

straightway the fountain of her blood was dried up, and she felt in her body that she was healed of that plague." Mark 5:25-30

"...when she had heard of Jesus..." Mark 5:27

Notice, it was what she heard about Jesus that made all the difference. Remember, faith comes by hearing. Her faith was literally activated and inspired to reach for her miracle. This is the power of testimonies.

MY FAITH WAS INSPIRED

Someone shared her testimony in an open revival I attended some years ago and my faith rose up and I got my miracle. And here is the testimony:

May 15th, 1980, was the actual day I gave my life to Jesus Christ in a powerful crusade conducted by Apostle Timothy Obadare in Akure city, the state capital of Ondo State in Nigeria, West Africa in a Ministry called World Soul-winning Evangelistic Ministries.

Prior to the time I came to this crusade, I had a spirit of infirmity in my body walking up and down my system and was affecting me terribly. I had been to many places to get it resolved but to no avail and instead it became worse. But the very week I attended this crusade, I began to witness God in action; there was a miracle galore. I was stunned, could God heal people? Was the time of miracle not passed with the early Apostles? Was speaking in tongues still in existence? These were the questions that flooded my heart. In a denominational church, I was coming from, I had been indoctrinated that the time of miracle had passed with the early Apostles and speaking in tongues was forbidden and that God could heal occasionally if He wished. On the last weekend of May 1980, during the revival time in the evening, a woman came out to share her own testimony.

In her testimony, I discovered that she had a similar situation of affliction I was going through and as a matter of fact her own was triple mine. This woman was full of joy, jubilating and praising God for her total deliverance.

As soon as I heard the testimony of this lady, my faith was fired up and I just jumped to a conclusion that I had been healed, and that was it. And instead of me wishing to be healed or praying to God to heal me, I started thanking Him for my healing. I was healed and I had a powerful encounter with God. I became a new creation and my life had never been the same again.

If you get the right word and meditate on them along with inspiring testimonies, your faith will be stirred up. And I can tell you, once your faith is stirred up, you are ready to receive your miracles. Once your faith is anchored on the word, no mountain will be able to stop you!

GEAR UP YOUR FAITH!

Usually, when a difficult situation arises, we all want our faith to be up and doing. We want our faith to be instantly geared up to respond. Unfortunately, it doesn't. A lot of times, people are defeated not because the challenge they are facing is too much for them, but because their faith is weak. The Bible says, if you fail in times of adversity, your strength is small (Proverbs 24:10). The adversity is not the problem, your strength level it.

So, what testimonies seek to do is get our faith adrenaline rushing, to present the picture of possibilities so that we can be inspired to release our faith. I tell you what, if you can hook up with the power of testimonies, you will see your faith soar into new heights of victory. In essence, our faith can be inspired or fired up towards our desires. And one of the ways to do that is through the power of testimonies. In fact, we defeat the enemy by the words of our testimonies.

The book of Revelation 12:11 says, "...they overcame him by the blood of the Lamb and by the word of their testimony, and they did not love their lives to the death."

Believe me, testimonies are powerful not only to literally get your faith off the ground but to inspire you to your next level of breakthrough. That will be your story!

6

THE POWER OF GOD'S WORD

The word of God is the bedrock of our faith. Without a strong word foundation, you cannot have faith. The word of God is the boundary of God's commitment to man. This is why God can only throw His weight behind what He has promised. Having a strong foundation in the word is, therefore, the greatest advantage of your faith walk. If you want the kind of faith that delivers victory every time, anchor your faith on the power of the word of God, because once God says it, then He is committed to doing it.

"God is not a man, that he should lie; neither the son of man, that he should repent: hath he said, and shall he not do it? or hath he spoken, and shall he not make it good?" Numbers 23:19

"And being fully persuaded that, what He had promised, He was able also to perform." Romans 4:21

FAITH COMES BY HEARING

How do I get faith? How exactly does faith work? You may ask. Or how can I apply my faith to produce results in my life? If you know how to acquire something and how it works; you have the key to making it happen every time you want it to happen. That means you are no longer waiting on it to happen of its own volition. It is the same with faith; there is a specific way to acquire faith.

"So then faith cometh by hearing, and hearing by the word of God." Romans 10:17

Although that scripture tells us emphatically that faith is the result of hearing the word of God. We must realize that it is not necessarily the mere hearing of the word that births faith but hearing the word with your heart. In other words, Faith is a product of divine revelation of the word of God.

Notice, in the scripture above the word "hearing" appears twice. Firstly, that emphasizes the place of hearing the word on the birthing of faith. Secondly, there is a difference between the first and the second hearing.

The first hearing refers to merely getting information with your mind. But then there is the second hearing— which points to heating with your heart. It is a hearing produced by understanding. Apostle Paul in his epistle to the Ephesians church refers to it as "the eyes of your understanding being enlightened..." (Ephesians 1:18). So, obviously, this speaks of revelation knowledge.

The power of God's word is NEVER released until there is revelation knowledge.

This is the kind of knowledge produced from the education of the heart. I mean, the enlightenment of the recreated human spirit. Once this kind of knowledge is unveiled, faith is unleashed and the power of God's word manifests. With the first hearing, the information is at the mental realm, but with the second realm, there is insight. That means the word has entered the heart. This explains the words of David in the one hundred and nineteenth psalm:

"The entrance of thy words giveth light; it giveth understanding unto the simple." Psalm 119:130

The word "light" here stands for revelation-knowledge or insight into the word of God. You cannot have faith apart from the revealed word of God. It is possible to receive information only as a mental accent. That means, you agree with what the word of God says at the mental level. But that doesn't necessarily mean that you have faith. Faith comes when the word goes beyond your mind and enters into your spirit. It is like light, permeating an arena of darkness. The Bible word for that is rightly so—entrance.

Revelation is, therefore, the mother of faith. If there is no revelation of the word, your faith has no basis and therefore would not produce results.

PRAYER EDUCATES YOUR HEART

This is why prayer is very important in developing your faith. Knowing about God alone does not birth faith, it is mere information; it is called theology—the study about God. Many people know a lot about God, yet they don't even know God. They only have head-knowledge, which they acquired through the physical senses, through reading. But whiles reading or learning will educate your mind, prayer is what will educate your heart (spirit). And one of the beautiful things about prayer is that when you pray, you will awaken the anointing; and it is the anointing that truly educates our spirit.

"But ye have an unction from the Holy One, and ye know all things...But the anointing which ye have received of him abideth in you, and ye need not that any man teach you: but as the same anointing teacheth you of all things, and is truth, and is no lie, and even as it hath taught you, ye shall abide in him."1 John 2:20,27

In fact, one of the promises Jesus made to his disciples before he ascended to heaven was that He would send the person of the Holy Spirit. And one of the many ministries of the Holy Spirit is to teach the believer.

"Howbeit when He, the Spirit of truth, is come, He will guide you into all truth: for He shall not speak of Himself; but whatsoever He shall hear, that shall He speak: and He will show you things to come." John 16:13

Prayer is a shortcut to divine revelation. It is the precursor to faith. When you pray, especially in tongues, you open yourself to the ministry of the Holy Spirit causing divine revelations to open to you.

Remember, the letter killeth, but it is the spirit that gives life—life to the written word of God. Prayer removes the veil blocking us from seeing things the way they are, bringing us face to face with the living word.

"But even unto this day, when Moses is read, the vail is upon their heart. Nevertheless, when it shall turn to the Lord, the vail shall be taken away. Now the Lord is that Spirit: and where the Spirit of the Lord is, there is liberty." 2 Corinthians 3:15-17

In fact, it is really this revelation that is made possible by the ministry of the Holy Spirit that brings about a transformation in our lives.

"But we all, with open face beholding as in a glass the glory of the Lord, are changed into the same image from glory to glory, even as by the Spirit of the Lord." 2 Corinthians 3:18

The word of God is the authorized channel of transformation, but the word cannot carry out that function effectively without the ministry of the Spirit, facilitated by prayer. This is also why the apostle Paul prayed earnestly for his converts.

"Wherefore I also, after I heard of your faith in the Lord Jesus, and love unto all the saints, Cease not to give thanks for you, making mention of you in my prayers; That the God of our Lord Jesus Christ, the Father of glory may give unto you the spirit of wisdom and revelation in the knowledge of Him: The eyes of your understanding being enlightened; that ye may know what is the hope of His calling, and what the riches of the glory of His inheritance in the saints." Ephesians 1:15-18

ENGAGE THE FORCE OF MEDITATION

Another very vital way of gaining insight or revelation is through meditation. Meditating the promises of God will birth faith. Once you have gotten the word on the area of your need or challenge, spend time meditating on it.

Mediation is spiritual digestion and assimilation. The same way your body feeds on and assimilates physical food, your spirit man feeds on and assimilates the word of God. Revelation occurs when there is spiritual assimilation. The Bible says man shall not live by bread (physical food) alone but by every word that proceeds out of the mouth of God (Luke 4:4). Truly, the word is food to the spirit.

"Moreover He said unto me, Son of man, eat that thou findest; eat this roll, and go speak unto the house of Israel. So I opened my mouth, and he caused me to eat that roll. And he said unto me, Son of man, cause thy belly to eat, and fill thy bowels with this roll that I give thee. Then did

I eat it; and it was in my mouth as honey for sweetness."
Ezekiel 3:1-3

Oh, I love how verse one is rendered In the Message translation:

"...son of man, eat what you see. Eat this book...As I opened my mouth, he gave me the scroll to eat, saying, "son of man, eat this book that I am giving you. Make a full meal of it". So I ate it. It tasted so good—just like honey." Ezekiel 3:1-3 (MSG)

In the book of John, Jesus declared, "I am the bread of life..." John 6:48

And remember, Jesus is the living word of God—the word made flesh (John 1:14)

Of course, the book he was referring to is the Bible. In other words, the word of God revealed in scripture is the real food for the spirit.

In eating, three major things happen; you chew, you swallow, and you digest (assimilate) what you have eaten. When it comes to spiritual food, meditation is chewing, which facilitates digestion and assimilation of the nutrients (revelation) into the (spirit). Now once assimilation occurs, that revelation becomes a part of you.

Meditation is the Hebrew word, "*śûach*" found in Genesis 24:63, which means to muse, commune, or speak. Also in the book of Joshua 1:8, we see another Hebrew word, "*hâgâh*", which means to moan, growl, utter, muse, mutter, devise, roar, or imagine. Meditation is more than sitting down to think about the word, it also involves muttering it, speaking it, or roaring the word like a lion. Meditation is the key to spiritual wisdom.

"And Isaac went out to meditate in the field at the eventide: and he lifted up his eyes, and saw, and, behold, the camels were coming." Genesis 24:63

Meditation not only unlocks faith but is also a major key to success. And I mean, good success.

"This book of the law shall not depart out of thy mouth; but thou shalt meditate therein day and night, that thou mayest observe to do according to all that is written therein: for then thou shalt make thy way prosperous, and then thou shalt have good success." Joshua 1:8

Stand on God's promises.

With this understanding of how faith cones, you are thoroughly armed to take advance of your inheritance. Revelation knowledge is what empowers you and me to access everything that belongs to us in Christ.

"And now, brethren, I commend you to God, and to the word of his grace, which is able to build you up, and to give you an inheritance among all them which are sanctified." Acts 20:32

So, if you are going through a specific challenge in any area of your life, what you need to do is to get acquainted with God's promises regarding that area and begin to meditate on them until faith is born in your heart. If it's an issue with your finances or career, get a hold of God's word in that area. If you need healing or deliverance, simply go get healing scriptures and stay with them. As a student in college, you cannot be studying accounting, when you have a math test the next day. You have to focus on your area of need in order to birth faith in that area. That is how it works.

Do you remember the young man healed by Paul? This young man had been listening to Paul teach for a long time; but as soon as Paul sensed his faith, he lifted him up on his feet.

"And there sat a certain man at Lystra, impotent in his feet, being a cripple from his mother's womb, who never had walked: The same heard Paul speak: who steadfastly beholding him, and perceiving that he had faith to be healed, Said with a loud voice, Stand upright on thy feet. And he leaped and walked." Acts 14:8-10

But you know what, the secret was that he had faith to be healed, not faith to prosper or faith to be saved. He had faith to be healed. That means, Paul must have been teaching along that line, right? Faith comes in the area of your revelation.

The promises of God are the platform to stand on in placing a demand on the ability of God. When you have God's promises, you can rest assured of victory in every area of challenge, because God is faithful to His promises. "Let us hold fast the profession of our faith without wavering; (for He is faithful that promised;)" Hebrews 10:23. He has never failed before, and He will not start from you. He will not fail you!

7

ENGAGE IN FERVENT PRAYER

If you can keep faith alive, you can keep victory alive. If you can keep your faith vibrant, you can conquer any difficulty that may come your way, no matter how challenging it may seem. But to keep your faith alive, fervent prayer is required. It takes fervent prayer to maintain a vibrant spiritual life active enough to deliver results. It is the fervency of your prayer-life that determines the buoyancy of your faith-life. Not only that your prayer brings fresh revelations, but prayer also keeps your spirit buoyant. When prayer is consistent and effective, it keeps your faith bubbling with the divine life. You have to understand that the divine life is not an independent life. In other words, it needs to be consistently serviced to keep it working optimally. And the way to service your faith is through the combined ministry of the word and the ministry of the Holy Spirit—unlocked through prayer.

Prayer is a very powerful force both to unlock and release your faith. Prayer is also the avenue by which you can gain access to all of the resources of God. Fervent prayer can literally do the impossible. The only thing prayer can not do is what God cannot do. I wonder what that would be! Everything bows on the altar of fervent prayer. God's power is an inexhaustible resource, but it takes prayer to draw from it. Be it salvation, deliverance, or healing, it takes prayer to make them happen.

"Is any among you afflicted? let him pray. Is any merry? let him sing psalms. Is any sick among you? let him call for the elders of the church; and let them pray over him, anointing him with oil in the name of the Lord: And the prayer of faith shall save the sick, and the Lord shall raise him up; and if he has committed sins, they shall be forgiven him." James 5:13-15

It is only the prayer done by faith that can heal the sick. So prayer is the avenue for channeling our faith to get our needs met. God does not transact with dollars or pounds sterling; God only transacts by faith. Faith is God's kingdom currency, it is the currency of heaven; that faith is transacted with prayer. Like a balloon, your faith requires the substance generated in the place of prayer for it to be effective. In fact, it takes prayer to generate the power required to make things happen.

"...The effectual fervent prayer of a righteous man availeth much." James 5:16

And then verse 17, says "Elias was a man subject to like passions as we are, and he prayed earnestly that it might not rain: and it rained not on the earth by the space of three years and six months. And he prayed again, and the heaven gave rain, and the earth brought forth her fruit." James 5:17

KEEP YOUR PRAYER FIRE BURNING

So, fervent prayer is imperative to the execution of divine will on the earth. You are as powerful as your faith, but your faith is as powerful as your word-life and your prayer-life. The word alone is not enough to sustain the fire required to keep your faith in top gear. The reason you need to service your altar of prayer is to keep your faith alive. Prayer strengthens your faith. Without a vibrant prayer life, your faith will soon lay flat on the floor. The Bible tells us that the fire of prayer should never be allowed to go out.

"The fire shall ever be burning upon the altar; it shall never go out." Leviticus 6:13

You cannot walk effectively by faith until you understand how to pray. The carelessness of people who can't pray is what is stopping their faith from working. That is also what enthroned the flesh on their affair, causing them to be defeated. If your prayer life is working, your faith-life is likely to be working too. That means you will be rich in faith. If you are truly rich in faith, then you can convert it to meet any kind of need you may have through the instrumentality of prayer. But if you choose to drop your faith, you drop your life, because the Bible says "the just shall live by faith..." (Hebrews 10:28). If you choose to drop your faith through prayerlessness, you will find yourself dropping your victory as well.

ENERGIZE YOUR WORDS

The place of prayer is the place where supernatural energy is both generated and deployed to produce results. We have talked about the place of your words, but prayer is essential to make your words effective. In fact, there is a level of spiritual energy that must be contained in your words to carry it through to manifestation. It is a prayer that takes you beyond the word of faith to the spirit of faith. Mere confession takes a longer time to manifest; but through fervent prayer, power is generated. And as you boldly declare God's word into the atmosphere of the spirit generated through fervent prayer; it becomes a reality because your words carry enough spiritual energy to bring what you declare to pass. That was exactly what happened in the creation story of Genesis chapter one. So first, God allowed the spirit to move before declaring the word. The movement of the spirit that we see in Genesis chapter one is typical of the atmosphere and power generated when we pray fervently.

"In the beginning, God created heaven and earth. And the earth was without form and void, and darkness was upon the face of the deep. And the Spirit of God moved upon the face of the waters. And God said, Let there be light: and there was light." Genesis 1:1-3

It was as the word met the energy of the Spirit that creation leaped into manifestation. That is why prayer is very important for your faith to function effectively.

TEACH US TO PRAY

If you understand prayer and pray regularly, your faith will always be on point. Prayer was the only thing the disciples ever asked Jesus to teach them. They did not ask Jesus to teach them how to preach, teach, or cast out devils. In fact, they did not even ask him to teach them how to raise the dead, as powerful as that is. They only asked him to teach them how to pray, because they eventually figured out his secret. They knew that prayer was the secret of everything he did—I mean, virtually EVERYTHING! They watched Jesus heal the sick with ease, they saw him cleanse the lepers, cast out demons, and raise the dead. They witnessed mind-blowing miracles that made them stand in awe. But they knew that all that would not have been possible without the divine input brought to the table by a long, fervent, and consistent prayer life. That is how powerful prayer is. One prominent Jewish leader once said to Jesus, "...for no man can do these miracles that thou doest, except God be with him." John 3:2

They all knew that it was the supernatural, made available through prayer and fellowship, that made all the difference in the public ministry of Jesus. The truth is, we have to begin to value prayer as the early Christians did. They understood that it takes prayer to activate the ministry of the Holy Spirit in the life of the believer. Prayer is what provokes a fresh infilling of the Holy Spirit. Remember, you are baptized with the Holy Spirit once and for all, but you get to be re-filled with Holy Spirit again and again. It is not a new Holy Spirit, but the same Holy Spirit freshly poured on you. And this is made possible as you pray, especially when you pray in the spirit.

When the disciples of Jesus were threatened not to preach the gospel, their response was to pray that God would confirm the word with signs and wonders. Here was what happened as they prayed fervently to God:

"And now, Lord, behold their threatenings: and grant unto thy servants, that with all boldness they may speak thy word, By stretching forth thine hand to heal; and that signs and wonders may be done by the name of thy holy child Jesus. And when they had prayed, the place was shaken where they were assembled together; and they were all filled with the Holy Ghost, and they spake the word of God with boldness." Acts 4:29-31

Notice: "...when they prayed...they were filled with the Holy Spirit..."

PRAY IN THE SPIRIT

"Praying always with all prayer and supplication in the Spirit, and watching thereunto with all perseverance and supplication for all saints." Ephesians 6:18

The phrase, "...with all prayer..." can actually be rendered as: "with all kinds of prayer..." So, what it means is that we are to pray with all kinds of prayer.

Evidently, there are different kinds of prayers mentioned in the scripture, and you can choose anyone to deal with challenges as the case may be. There is the prayer of thanksgiving, consecration, the prayer of agreement, the prayer of faith, and so on. However, whichever one you choose to engage, it must be done in line with the Biblical recommendation of praying in the spirit. You cannot afford to make supplication in the flesh; if you do, not only that it will not be effective, it will not produce the required results. With the baptism of the Holy Spirit comes the divine ability to speak in other tongues. This is technically called the prayer language.

"And when the day of Pentecost fully came, they were all with one accord in one place. And suddenly there came a sound from heaven as of a rushing mighty wind, and it filled all the house where they were sitting. And there appeared unto them cloven tongues like as of fire, and it sat upon each of them. And they were all filled with the Holy Ghost, and began to speak with other tongues, as the Spirit gave them utterance." Acts 2:1-4

YOU HAVE HIS HOTLINE

Every believer who is truly baptized with the Holy Spirit has a prayer language by which he communicates directly to God. Praying in the spirit is like a hotline that reaches God directly. It may sound different for different people, but ultimately with it, a believer can communicate with God effectively. Speaking in other tongues is a very powerful way to pray effectively and unlock t he dynamic ability of God in us to cause changes not just in our personal, professional life, and in our circumstances; but also in the lives and circumstances of many others. Now, that you can speak in other tongues, you should endeavor to exercise your spirit in prayer regularly. The beautiful thing is that whenever you pray on other tongues, you build up your most Holy faith.

"But ye, beloved, building up yourselves on your most holy faith, praying in the Holy Ghost, Keep yourselves in the love of God..." Jude 20

When you pray in the Holy Spirit, you built up your other senses, thereby facilitating your walk of faith. The Bible says, "We walk by faith, not by sight." 2 Corinthians 5:7. The word, "sight" refers to sensory perception. So, we don't walk by our natural sense, but by our spiritual sense.

Another wonderful thing that happens when you pray is that your love is stirred up afresh; and when that happens, your faith is activated. Speaking in tongues keeps you in the love of God (Jude 21), thereby keeping your faith alive. Remember, the love of God is shed in our hearts by the Holy Ghost (Rom. 5:5), and "faith works by love." Hence, prayer empowers your love-life, and your love-life empowers your faith-life. Prayer is also how you deploy your faith to make spiritual withdraws from the unlimited resources of God's kingdom. Ultimately, it is the fervency of your prayer-life that determines the buoyancy of your faith-life.

Do you want your faith to work wonders, then never let the force of your faith run dry; never let your prayer account run dry. This is one of the greatest keys to the ever-winning faith life.

8

CONFESSION AND AFFIRMATION OF FAITH

As we conclude these 21 days prayer program, make the following faith affirmation loud and clear:

I follow after righteousness -Isaiah 51:1.

I am here from the rock which is Jesus

I have the life nature character mind of Christ -1 Corinthians 2:16.

Like Abraham the Lord has blessed and increased me -Isaiah 51:2.

The Lord will comfort my waste places -Isaiah 51:3.

The Lord will make my wilderness like that of the garden of Eden -Isaiah 51:3.

He will make my desert like the garden of the Lord -Isaiah 51:3.

God is not a man that He should lie nor a son of man that He should repent -Numbers 23:19.

Everything He has concerning me will be established.

The Lord has blessed me and my blessings can't be reversed -Numbers 23:20.

The Lord my God is with me and the shout of a king is among us -Numbers 23:21.

I have strength like a wild Ox

For there is no sorcery against me nor any divination against me shall prosper -Numbers 23:23.

It shall be said concerning me oh what the Lord has done -Psalm 66:7.

I'm no longer a slave to fear I am a child of God -Galatians 4:4-6.

My life is marked by excellence and integrity.

God abundance is surrounding my life today.

I'm not fearful over my financial future.

I will not doubt I will not worry -Philippians 4:7.

I'm in a household of faith and not in the dungeon of fear -Galatians 6:10.

I have the grace I need for today 2 Corinthians 12:9

God is directing my steps -Psalm 37:23.

I'm full of power strength and determination
-Micah 3:8

My household is flourishing and not failing.

My household isn't just surviving but thriving.

Nothing I face will be too much for me.

I will overcome every obstacle outlast every
challenge and come through every difficulty

God has a plan for my life. Jeremiah 29:11-13.

I'm a vessel of grace. Psalm 66:8.

I was prepared for glory before the world began.

The world is waiting for me. Romans 8:19.

The angels have been assigned as my servants.
Hebrews 1:14.

My failure today is not my destination. Psalm
145:14.

My defeat today is not my destination. Hebrews
12:3.

Any negative circumstance is only a transit point.
Romans 8:18.

Until I arrive at my destination I have not arrived.
Philippians 1:6.

I'm God's choice on no merit of mine. Ephesians 1:4

By grace I have been saved it's a gift of God Ephesians 2:8.

I'm God's chosen for the hour.

I'm God's choice for this generation -1 Peter 2:9.

I'm God's favorite for this time.

I have stepped into God's prepared plan-Jeremiah 1:5.

I'm product of divine election God's choice and that settles it -2 Peter 1:4 and 1 Peter 2:9.

I'm called to glory and virtue-2 Peter 1:3

I'm called to greatness and honor -Isaiah 61:6-7.

I'm not called to reproach and poverty -Isaiah 50:7.

I'm called to walk in authority and dominion -Luke 10:19.

I'm called to wealth -2 Peter 1:3 and Galatians 3:13-14.

I'm called to possess an inheritance -Acts 26:18.

I'm called to be the head and not the tail -Deuteronomy 28:13.

I'm called to signs and wonders -Isaiah 8:18.

Blessed shall I be in the city -Deuteronomy 28:3.

Blessed shall I be in the country -Deuteronomy 28:3.

Blessed shall be the fruit of my body. Deuteronomy 28:4.

Blessed shall be the produce of my ground. Deuteronomy 28:4.

Blessed shall be works of my hands. Deuteronomy 28:8.

Blessed shall I be when I come in. Deuteronomy 28:6.

Blessed shall I be when I go out. Deuteronomy 28:6.

The Lord will cause my enemies who rise against me to be defeated before my face. Deuteronomy 28:7.

They shall come out against me one way and flee before me seven ways -Deuteronomy 28:7.

The Lord will command the blessings on me and in my storehouses. Deuteronomy 28:8.

The Lord will open to me his treasures -Deuteronomy 28:12.

The heaven will give the rain to my land in its season. Deuteronomy 28:12

The heavens will bless all the work of my hands. Deuteronomy 28:12.

I will lend to many nations I will not borrow. Deuteronomy 28:12

I will be above only I will not be beneath. Deuteronomy 28:13.

Every word I have spoken shall be established.

I will do exceedingly abundantly more than I can think or imagine -Ephesians 3:20.

ACKNOWLEDGMENTS

I want to acknowledge my spiritual father, Apostle Timothy Obadare, who has gone into glory, through whom I gave my life to Jesus on May 15th, 1980.

Other spiritual mentors I owe a great gratitude to are, General Overseer of Deeper Life, W.F Kumuyi, G.O of The Redeem Christian Church of God, Pastor E.A Adeboye, Bishop David Oyedepo, Winners Chapel, Kenneth Hagin Sr, Oral Roberts, to mention just a few. Through their teachings and writings, I have been guided on the right path. I will always be thankful to them.

I appreciate our lovely children, Dorcas, Ruth, Joshua and Christy, they have made us proud. I decree they will all fulfill destinies in Jesus mighty name.

I am grateful to all my ministers, workers and members at International Way of Life Ministries, Houston Texas for believing in the call of God over my life. You all are the best. I'm so proud of what we have been able to accomplish together.

I will like to acknowledge all members of Greater Houston

Ministers Fellowship, whom friendship and fellowship have continue to be a blessing to me. May the Lord uphold all of us together.

I am thankful to my dear friend, Bishop Simeon Agbolabori. Thank you for always supporting and cheering me on in everything I do. You are a true definition of loyalty.

This book is a dream come true through the consulting help, advice, and professional inputs of Pastor Gbenga Showunmi and his team at Cornerstone Concept and Publishing. They are fantastic publishers and they have already fired me up.

It will not be fair if I don't acknowledge Pastor Christy Ogbeide. This woman of God called me some years back and she asked "Pastor Osho Where is the book the Lord told me you are writing?" She was actually the third person sent to me by God that I will write a book.

The book is now in your hands; enjoy it as you progress.

ABOUT THE AUTHOR

David Osho preaches the undiluted word of GOD. He is known for his praying life and miracles happen when he ministers by the grace of GOD. He believes in miracles. The mandate God gave him is to liberate mankind from the suffering and bondages of Satan through the power in the Word of GOD.

Pastor Osho believes the age of miracle has not passed. He is the founder and the senior pastor of international way of life ministry based in Houston Texas. He has been in the ministry for four decades. He received his doctorate degree in divinity from Juliana King University, Houston Texas U.S.A.

He is happily married to his lovely wife, "Honey Me," Pastor Esther Olufunke Osho and their marriage is blessed with four children - Dorcas, Ruth, Joshua and Christy.

CPSIA information can be obtained
at www.ICGtesting.com
Printed in the USA
LVHW080708280622
722184LV00011B/479